The Genius of Frank E. Campbell

The Story of How One Man Changed Funeral Service and Unwittingly Set the Stage for Movie Stars

TODD W. VAN BECK

The Family Coat of Arms of
FRANK E. CAMPBELL

MR. FRANK E. CAMPBELL

1872 – 1934

DEDICATION

This book is dedicated to:
Mr. Eugene R. Schultz and **Mr. George M. Amato**,
former presidents of Frank E. Campbell, The Funeral Chapel.
Both gentlemen are consummate funeral professionals who contributed
manifestly to the nobility and improvement of our beloved profession.

CONTENTS

1	Beginnings	Pg #2
2	New York City	Pg #4
3	The Rev. Stephen Merritt	Pg #6
4	The Merritt-Campbell Split	Pg #13
5	The Funeral Church	Pg #17
6	Frank E. Campbell Ambulance	Pg #20
7	Professor Lina D. Odou	Pg #22
8	66th Street & Broadway	Pg #29
9	Frank E. Campbell - The Man	Pg #34
10	Creativity and Innovation	Pg #36
11	A Day at The Funeral Church	Pg #38
12	Good Works	Pg #42
13	Valentino	Pg #44
14	The Final Days	Pg #53
15	Rest in Peace Mr. Campbell - ???	Pg #55
16	Mr. Campbell's Ghost	Pg #56
17	Eulogy	Pg #58

INTRODUCTION

Talk about branding! Frank E. Campbell. The name says it all, well at least with New Yorkers and funeral professionals around the world.

Walk down any street in the boroughs of New York City and ask anybody you meet this question, "Name a funeral home in Manhattan?" Chances are very good that the response will be, "Frank E. Campbell."

This author was dining in the Oak Room at the Plaza Hotel in New York City several years ago and I asked the bartender, "Do you know a funeral director in the city?" He responded immediately without hesitation, "Sure, Frank E. Campbell."

Now ask any funeral director, "Who is the most famous funeral director ever?" The response will most often be: Frank E. Campbell.

Added to all this is that the policy of the New York Times, when they run obituaries of the rich and famous, is to NOT mention specific funeral home names, unless the funeral is being conducted by Frank E. Campbell.

The clientele of Frank E. Campbell reads like a veritable who's who of the rich and famous. Here is a very small idea of celebrity and social luminaries who have been cared for by Frank E. Campbell, The Funeral Chapel: Elizabeth Arden, Yul Brenner, James Cagney, Jacqueline Kennedy, Robert F. Kennedy, John Lennon, Judy Garland, J.C. Penny, Mae West, and of course, Rudolph Valentino.

Today the Frank E. Campbell building at 81st and Madison Avenue in Manhattan is very discrete and draws little attention to itself. The founder however, Frank E. Campbell, was not discrete at times, and certainly was an expert at drawing attention to himself and his firm. Frank E. Campbell is still the reigning funeral home in Manhattan, but the man himself has been dead for over 80 years. It is time that his story be told, and what a story it is. We begin by asking some interesting questions.

Who was Frank E. Campbell? How did he become a funeral director, and how did this one funeral director attract such a lustrous clientele? What was Frank E. Campbell like as a real live human being, and why was Mr. Campbell's remains not permanently buried until almost seventy five years after his death? This work attempts to answer these and a myriad of other questions about the life and career of Frank E. Campbell.

In the annals of funeral service history it is generally conceded and accepted by students of the subject that one man, Frank E. Campbell, Mortician (he himself preferred mortician to funeral director) produced one of the most profound and lasting impacts on American funeral service practices in the late 19th, and the early 20th century.

Reader, meet Frank E. Campbell.

1. BEGINNINGS

PLANTING THE SEEDS OF THE FUNERAL "CELEBRITY"

This is the life story of Frank E. Campbell who could easily be called one of the only true funeral celebrities that America has produced. Other funeral directors have left their mark – but to claim the status of being a celebrity is very unique in the funeral service profession.

The use of the word "celebrity" in the same sentence about a person, now long dead, who was of all things an "undertaker" might strike many readers as odd. Aren't undertakers usually portrayed as unusual and even creepy people?

We usually think of celebrities, certainly not as undertakers, but as movie stars, members of the Hollywood elite, or members of the legitimate stage on Broadway, names emblazoned in lights on the grand marque. We don't usually think of a mortician as being part of the world of the Hollywood elite or the New York stage. However, to arrive at such a biased attitude would be a mistake. Frank E. Campbell was an indelible force to reckon with in both worlds of film and the stage, and he was much more. As we will see, for a period of a little over thirty years, the influence of Frank E. Campbell was felt in the business world, the entertainment world, the education world, and in the world of charities and good works.

EARLY HISTORY

Frank Ellis Campbell was born in the small downstate town of Camp Point, Illinois on July 4, 1872. Camp Point, Illinois had a population of 1300 people when Frank E. Campbell was born.

Frank E. Campbell shared the exact birth day and year with President Calvin Coolidge. Throughout his lifetime Mr. Campbell used the coincidence of his birthday, and that of President Coolidge and the Fourth of July being on the same day, as a grand opportunity to host spectacular birthday parties over the years for both himself and the nation. Adding to this festive atmosphere was Mr. Campbell's own gregarious personality and the event was anticipated annually by many.

The account of Mr. Campbell's life is, without exaggeration, a Horatio Alger, rags to riches story. Campbell started life with one harsh fact: the Campbell family was poor.

Frank's father George Salon Campbell was the son of Alexander and Elizabeth Campbell. His mother, Malvina T. Frazell, was born in 1838 in Adams County, Illinois and died in 1926 in New York City having moved there later to be with her son and his family.

Frank had two sisters: Flora Evangeline who married Edward Volney Peters, and Catherine (Kate) who later married William Lavini of Camp Point. Frank also had a brother Charles who died at the age 27. The early years of Frank E. Campbell are sketchy and over his lifetime he was extremely reticent about recalling childhood memories.

Throughout his life Frank E. Campbell worshipped his mother Malvina and he doted on her throughout her life. Campbell did credit his mother with teaching him the benefits of a solid religious foundation. These religious teachings served him well in his professional and personal life.

One early account says that Frank E. Campbell had to go to work at the tender age of 12 because his father had died.

Frank E. Campbell attended public school in Camp Point, and while in school he became employed by a local undertaker who also manufactured brick and sold building materials along with ice and coal.

Frank made $1.00 a day. He cut raw timber for the making of furniture and caskets.

In the latter part of the 19th century it was not uncommon for the local undertaker to be involved in a variety of other business activities ranging from selling furniture, to operating livery stables, to even selling farm implements and hardware.

During this time Campbell officiated at many funerals and burials and he also built coffins, as well as making furniture and delivering ice and coal. Frank E. Campbell claimed that he conducted his first funeral on his own at the age of 18.

Frank E. Campbell worked as a undertaker in Camp Point for five years, and while in this employment became an expert in grading lumber – a talent that he would later put to excellent use in the interior decorating of his own facility, which became one of the most modern and beautiful mortuaries in the world.

2. NEW YORK CITY

In 1892, at age of 20, Frank E. Campbell left Camp Point and made his way to the largest city in the United States – New York. Just why he picked New York City is still a mystery. Possibly he had a young man's fancy to go out and see the world.

FRANK E. CAMPBELL

We do know that Mr. Campbell later in life shared that he felt that Camp Point funeral customs were stale, out of date, and boring. Frank E. Campbell took issue with the old fashioned kind of undertaker who was usually located in a downtown storefront and who sold furniture, made cabinets and even possibly operated a livery stable. In Illinois, late 19th century funerals, like most other places, were cookie cutter types of ceremonies, the same prayers, the same hymns and the same procedures. Frank E. Campbell concluded that funerals in the latter part of the 19th century were boring, and as his life would attest if Frank E. Campbell was anything he was NOT boring - so off to the biggest city in the United States he went – New York City.

Throughout his career Mr. Campbell rebelled at funeral practices that were short on service and short on creativity. He detested old fashioned service practices, and his career proved that innovative and creative funeral service is precisely what the general public is attracted to.

From the beginning of his career in New York City, Frank E. Campbell's notion of what represented the true mark of a service oriented funeral home was both remarkable and lasting.

At the time Frank E. Campbell moved to New York City, most of the undertaking establishments were little more than store front operations. Funerals were almost always held in homes, or more particularly in New York, in apartment houses.

Because of this situation most undertaking establishments in New York City were casket warehouses, hearse garages, horse stables and offices.

This drawing represents the typical storefront New York City undertaking establishments in 1885. These illustrations accompanied a newspaper article entitled "Mankind's Last Friend."

S. MERRITT HOOK.

New York City was a unique place to conduct funerals. In rural Illinois, where Mr. Campbell had come from, people generally lived in single family homes. However, in New York City people lived in apartments, private residential hotels (the predecessor of condominiums), mansions, town homes and of course tenements for the poor.

Large outside yards and lawns were unheard of. The number of New Yorker's inhabitants per square mile could be hundreds, and in the poorer sections of the city, even thousands.

In the cramped and over populated environment of New York City death was more problematic than could possibly be imagined, and this reality created logistic and organizational nightmares for most New York City undertakers.

Since elevators were still rare, getting caskets and all the necessary funeral equipment up flights of stairs to prepare and set up for an apartment funeral was an engineering feat. Getting caskets into an apartment most often necessitated the services of a carpenter who would remove a window or widen a doorway to accommodate the casket. Some undertakers actually kept carpenters on payroll to be called in at a moment's notice. Frank E. Campbell had contracted for the services of a safe moving company to use their heavy moving equipment to get a casket in a high rise New York City apartment. It was not an uncommon site to see a casket dangling 30 stories above the street in mid-air.

Transporting and getting the necessary funeral equipment, folding chairs, flower stands, background draperies, embalming equipment, and the myriad of other funeral items from the undertakers place of business to the place where the actual funeral would take place was hard, demanding, intense physical labor and mentally taxing.

It was into this unsophisticated and paralyzed funeral service environment that Frank E. Campbell arrived.

Immediately upon his arrival Frank E. Campbell obtained employment with the most prestigious and well-known undertaking establishment in New York City – The Stephen Merritt Burial Company.

3. THE REV. STEPHEN MERRITT

There was a time in the long and rich history of the funeral profession that few funeral directing firms in the United States could make claim to a more colorful and influential history than that of the Stephen Merritt Undertaking Company, later known as the Stephen Merritt Burial & Cremation Company.

**THE REV. STEPHEN MERRITT, JR.
1833 – 1917**

The Merritt firm was established in 1846 by the elder Stephen Merritt (the father of the Rev. Stephen Merritt of this story). The elder Merritt was the sexton and undertaker at the 18th Street Methodist Episcopal Church in Manhattan. The Merritt Undertaking firm saw New York City grow from a small city in the 1840's, which was still dominated by the Old Dutch Knickerbocker influences, to the teeming metropolis that it had become by the time Frank E. Campbell arrived.

The Merritt firm conducted thousands of funerals, and in their day they were considered to be the funeral home for the rich and famous. Merritt's conducted the New York funeral portion for Senator Daniel Webster, for Senator Henry Clay, and in 1885 the Merritt firm was called to arrange and conduct the funeral for President Ulysses S. Grant when he died at Mount McGregor in Upstate New York.

Our Stephen Merritt, the son of the founder, was also an ordained clergy in the Methodist Episcopal Church. Merritt had graduated from Amenia Seminary in Duchess County, New York, and for most of his professional life he went by the title of the Rev. Stephen Merritt.

Rev. Stephen Merritt was well known in the metropolitan area of New York as being a man of sincere Christian charity.

Rev. Merritt also purchased scores of burial spaces at the Maple Grove Cemetery in Queens, New York where for decades he gave free burial spaces for the people he called "the worthy poor." In fact, to this day there is a section of Maple Grove Cemetery named the Stephen Merritt Circle where 199 adults and infants are interred through Rev. Merritt's kindness and generosity.

However, the good Rev. Merritt was known for another character trait which was not so attractive. Rev. Merritt was very willing to bring a lawsuit against anyone who he felt had crossed him and had done him wrong. Throughout his long life Rev. Merritt sued a steady stream of people. Rev. Merritt sued his relatives (even his son, also named Stephen Merritt), he sued former employees (including Frank E. Campbell), and he sued other funeral directors (particularly the Saratoga Springs undertaker who had participated in the funeral of President Grant). Rev. Merritt was in legal litigation in some form or another for most all of his adult life.

REV. STEPHEN MERRITT, PENCIL DRAWING
NEW YORK HERALD, 1909

In 1912, Rev. Merritt sued his own grandson who was also in funeral service and also named Stephen Merritt. Relationships became so tense that these ads were published to help the public distinguish between the feuding Merritt's.

STEPHEN MERRITT BURIAL ETC. CO. V. STEPHEN MERRITT CO., ET AL. 373

STEPHEN MERRITT BURIAL & CREMATION CO. V. STEPHEN MERRITT CO., et al.

Special Term, New York County, August 8, 1912.

TRADE-NAME.
The use by defendants of a trade-name colorably similar to that of the plaintiff in the same line of business, held to be wrongful and subject to injunction.

Hedges, Ely & Frankel, for plaintiff.
C. R. & C. U. Carruth, for defendants.

PAGE, J.—It is well settled that "every man has the absolute right to use his own name honestly in his own business, even though he may thereby incidentally interfere with and injure the business of another having the same name. In such

THE AD FROM MERRITT'S GRANDSON...ANOTHER STEPHEN MERRITT

**TAKE NOTICE!
STEPHEN MERRITT**
Is not connected, interested or associated with the Concern at 19th St. and 8th Av.
Only Addresses fi you want
Rev. Stephen Merritt
PERSONALLY
MAIN Estab., 223 8th Av., near 21st St.
S. L. BUCKINGHAM, Mgr.   Tel. 1200 Chelsea.
HARLEM Estab., 304 West 126th St.
H. S. WYNKOOP, Mgr.   Tel. 5700 Morningside.
UNDERTAKERS. PRIVATE CHAPELS.

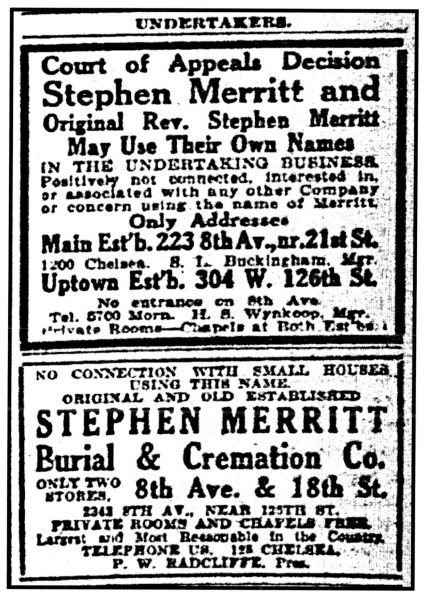

THESE ADS RAN TOGETHER – THE PUBLIC WAS BAFFLED AS TO WHO WAS WHO!

Yet for all Rev. Merritt's penchant for suing people, he was equally creative when it came to implementing high quality and very creative standards concerning his approach to funeral service. Take for example his invention of what he called the "Palace" funeral car.

Rev. Merritt invented a funeral omnibus that could accommodate mourners and the decedent in the same vehicle on the trip to the cemetery.

THE "PALACE" FUNERAL CAR
IN FRONT OF THE STEPHEN MERRITT BURIAL COMPANY

THIS BUILDING WOULD LATER BE THE FIRST LOCATION
OF FRANK E. CAMPBELL'S FUNERAL COMPANY

DETAILS OF REV. MERRITT'S "PALACE" FUNERAL CAR

Frank E. Campbell launched his New York City career at Stephen Merritt's where he was paid $10.00 a week and he slept in a room in the basement of the building. He sent $5.00 of his earnings back home to his mother and his family.

Frank E. Campbell was set on being a success and to that end he knew he had to learn the art and science of embalming, which was not being done much in Camp Point, Illinois. Mr. Campbell enrolled at the United States College of Embalming which was operated by the pioneer embalming professor Dr. Auguste Renouard.

Frank E. Campbell also sought training and education from the famed Civil War embalming-surgeon Dr. Thomas Holmes who lived across the East River in Brooklyn, and Campbell even traveled to Boston to get further embalming education from the well-known pioneer embalming educator, Professor A. Johnson Dodge, who was the President of the New England Institute of Anatomy, Embalming, Sanitary Science and Funeral Directing. Professor Dodge was also the founder of the Dodge Chemical Company.

Frank E. Campbell showed a life-long interest in the art and science of embalming, and as will be seen, he was the moving force in organizing and operating embalming colleges over his career.

Frank E. Campbell prospered working for Rev. Merritt and by 1898 Mr. Campbell had been made the General Manager of the Stephen Merritt organization, and was making the very impressive salary of $3,600.00 annually. This made Mr. Campbell the highest paid undertaker in New York City.

However, the situation at Stephen Merritt's was about to change significantly for Mr. Campbell, and not for the good.

Rev. Stephen Merritt was a complicated man. He was one contradiction after another. He was a devoted Christian and also an ordained clergyman. In his role as a clergyman, he founded the Nyack Children's Home (which was a well-known orphanage of the time), and the Bowery Mission where Rev. Merritt lead a project to feed up to 2000 of poor, disenfranchised New Yorkers every day.

For fourteen years Rev. Merritt was the publisher and editor of his own Christian magazine called the "King's Messenger" which at its peak had a circulation of over 40,000. Rev. Merritt was also active in numerous Masonic orders and participated regularly in the charitable works of that fraternal organization.

But . . . there was another side to Rev. Merritt's character which caused him, and many others, a lifetime of trouble.

For all his generous humanitarian efforts to be of service to humanity, Rev. Stephen Merritt could also be mean spirited, vindictive and petty. Then added to his cantankerousness, Rev. Merritt was a horrible businessman. Unfortunately, Rev. Merritt had no skill in handling money.

Throughout his long life and career not only was Rev. Merritt embroiled in one lawsuit after another, he also stood at the door of bankruptcy on several occasions.

Rev. Merritt greeted 1900, the turn of the century, by being in financial trouble again. And this time Rev. Merritt was in big financial trouble! Here is what happened.

Rev. Merritt had moved his original undertaking establishment which he and his father had operated, from West 14th Street to a larger more suitable facility located on West 23rd Street in the Chelsea District of Manhattan. It was at this location where Frank E. Campbell started his career in New York, and was ultimately promoted as the General Manager.

Rev. Merritt owed so many creditors, and was behind in so many payments, that for once the lawsuit tables were turned and now it was Rev. Merritt who was being sued. Rev. Merritt was being sued by his creditors and in the end, Merritt's creditors prevailed and won control of the Stephen Merritt Undertaking Company.

4. THE MERRITT-CAMPBELL SPLIT

The first thing the creditors did was remove Frank E. Campbell as the General Manager. However, word on the street was that there were backroom shenanigans going on between Merritt's creditors, the lawyers, and Frank E. Campbell.

Within weeks of the creditors taking over the Stephen Merritt Undertaking Company, and the removal of Frank E. Campbell, the creditors and their lawyers announced they had arrived at an entirely new business plan.

The creditors and lawyers happily announced that they had located someone who was highly qualified to manage the Merritt Company and who agreed to sublet the property on West 23rd Street. This new person was to receive a $6,000.00 annual salary.

The creditors were happy with this announcement and they breathed a sigh of relief, because under the new management - by this new highly qualified person – they would over time get them all money Rev. Merritt owed them. It appeared to be a capital idea!

There was one small surprise in this plan. The highly qualified person who the creditors had sublet the old Merritt building to, was none other than Frank E. Campbell.

When news of this agreement reached Rev. Merritt, he was absolutely stunned and blindsided! Rev. Merritt was furious and stated, "Why, they just fired Campbell not a month ago!" However, the deed was done.

Frank E. Campbell moved into the very building where just a short time before he had been General Manager, and into the location where he had been sacked. Stephen Merritt's name came down and Frank E. Campbell's name went up, and the Merritt/Campbell feud was born. This feud would end only with the death of Rev. Stephen Merritt in 1917.

In 1900, West 23rd was one of the major thoroughfares in New York City. The location was perfect for launching Frank E. Campbell's vision for innovative and creative funeral service, and he lost no time in putting his ideas into action. The creditors were paid in full, and once this task was completed Frank E. Campbell never looked back.

For his entire career Mr. Campbell had a gift for interior decorating, and with this talent in hand he started redecorating the West 23rd St. property in earnest. He filled the building with live palm trees, with priceless works of art, and hung monumental tapestries throughout the building.

Frank E. Campbell introduced the then new concept of offering "slumber rooms" for the public to view the dead. Now not a viewing at a private New York home or apartment, but now right in the premises of Frank E. Campbell.

New Yorker's were intrigued by the idea of going to the undertaker's facility to hold the wake instead of being subjected to the monumental task and hard work of getting everything arranged at the home or apartment for a funeral. New Yorker's quickly discovered that the "new" idea of using Frank E. Campbell's facility for everything was much easier, and everyone agreed that the Frank E. Campbell facility was ten times nicer than the average New Yorkers private abode.

Frank E. Campbell installed the first embalming/preparation room/care center in New York, and within two years the number of home embalming had dropped significantly.

Mr. Campbell added beautifully designed offices where funeral arrangements could be made in comfort and private, and he even introduced a newfangled notion that he called a "casket selection room" where the public could actually see, touch and examine the actual casket they would be using for their decedent, instead of catalogs.

In 1900, New York City had hundreds of "undertakers" but not one of them had seen anything like the funeral facility and level of funeral service excellence that was being developed rapidly by Frank E. Campbell. Frank E. Campbell would be at this 23rd St. location for seventeen years.

And this was just the beginning.

FRANK E. CAMPBELL AS A YOUNG FUNERAL DIRECTOR STARTING HIS CAREER AT THE WEST 23RD STREET LOCATION – THE FORMER STEPHEN MERRITT BUILDING

FRANK E. CAMPBELL "THE FUNERAL CHURCH" ON WEST 23RD STREET, MANHATTAN

Not only did Frank E. Campbell possess a skill in interior design and decorating, he was a natural at promotional and advertising creativity and innovation. Here is an example.

Prior to Frank E. Campbell few newspapers in the city ran paid death notices. Newspapers ran full length obituaries, but these obituaries almost never contained information about the location, time, and schedule of the actual funeral. The newspapers had concluded that the general public didn't need this information. Most newspapers at the time reasoned that old-fashioned word of mouth had always been the way that deaths had been announced in New York neighborhoods. The newspapers always depended on the gossip trail to spread the word when and where a funeral would take place. The newspapers also felt strongly that only certain important and famous people deserved to have an obituary printed, and the newspaper editors would determine who was important and famous.

Frank E. Campbell changed this practice.

With great delicacy and political acumen, Frank E. Campbell approached the editorial staffs of the major New York City newspapers and made the proposal that the newspaper actually sell paid death notice space. These "paid death notices" would give a brief sketch of the deceased but would focus and place emphasis on the time and location of the funeral.

Frank E. Campbell judiciously told the newspaper editors that this "paid death notice" service should be open to everyone who was willing to pay the newspaper, and not just the rich and famous who the newspaper editors declared deserved a printed obituary. The newspapers also would determine just how much the charge would be for these "paid death notices."

Most every New York newspaper took to the idea, and over time Frank E. Campbell's idea changed the way most every newspaper across the entire country handled paid death notices.

Frank E. Campbell also initiated the new idea that the funeral home would never close. At Frank E. Campbell's the front door on 23rd Street was opened 24 hours a day, 365 days a year. Anybody could walk in at any time and receive instant attention.

Over the next seventeen years, the number of bereaved families that were being served by Frank E. Campbell increased over eight times from what Rev. Merritt had been serving out of the same location. By 1917 Frank E. Campbell was conducting over 1000 funerals per year.

Frank E. Campbell

5. THE FUNERAL CHURCH

In 1905, Frank E. Campbell constructed the first formal funeral chapel in New York City, and he christened his funeral home, as "The Funeral Church." Frank E. Campbell composed at this time his famous professional credo: **"To create a service so sublimely beautiful, in an atmosphere of complete harmony, as to alleviate the sorrow of parting, is to render a service to mankind."**

The Funeral Church was astounding. The chapel in The Funeral Church was a miniature of a church. It had stained glass windows, a large pipe organ, mahogany pews and seating for two hundred and sixty-five with side seating for another two hundred.

The Funeral Church was a masterpiece of creativity. The chapel was on the second floor of the building, and a special elevator had been designed to lower the casket to the first floor. Throughout the entire building were priceless works of art. In time, The Funeral Church became not only a destination for the mourners of New York City, it became a destination for art connoisseurs, and even out-of-town tourists who appreciated fine art.

The Funeral Church chapel was dedicated on November 1, 1905 by the Rev. Dr. David Burrell of the Marble Collegiate Church, and the Rev. Dr. Charles L. Goodell of Calvary Methodist Episcopal Church.

To this day old timers in New York City will still refer to the Frank E. Campbell funeral establishment as The Funeral Church. Where did Frank E. Campbell get this very unusual name for a funeral home?

Here is the story. Central to Frank E. Campbell's tremendous advertising and promotional success of The Funeral Church was the employment of an advertising genius by the name of **Dr. Berthold A. Baer (1867 – 1924)**.

Dr. Baer composed the most famous of the Frank E. Campbell ads which described "The Funeral Church" as "A Church Without Spire or Belfry." The content of this ad explains the basis for the funeral service concept of The Funeral Church.

Dr. Baer was originally an eye surgeon from Philadelphia who became a well-known writer on the subject of death. It was Dr. Baer who is credited giving Frank E. Campbell the idea to call the funeral facility The Funeral Church.

Dr. Baer served for a time as the General Manager of the Frank E. Campbell establishment.

Frank E. Campbell used Dr. Baer's writing talents extensively in writing advertising copy for the funeral establishment. Dr. Baer's soothing words about death and the value and benefit of pre-planning for funerals were among the earliest mortuary advertising efforts in America. Dr. Baer was also a lyricist and composer and wrote the 1920's hit song "Don't Say Goodbye; Kiss Me Goodbye, But Don't Say Goodbye."

Frank E. Campbell was a funeral professional who was absolutely dedicated to advertising. For years one of his ads boldly declared that at The Funeral Church No deserving poor refused."

This is the script of the famous ad "The Church Without a Spire or Belfry."

FUNERAL DIRECTORS. | FUNERAL DIRECTORS.

The Church Without Spire or Belfry
By DR. BERTHOLD A. BAER

Thousands have asked and often I have wondered why Frank E. Campbell had named his institution for burial and cremation, Broadway at 66th Street, "The Funeral Church."

So I asked him.

"About twenty-five years ago," said Mr. Campbell, "the New York Tribune sent a journalist 'to write up' my place, at that time located on West 23d Street. I was the first so-called 'undertaker' who dared to extensively advertise in daily papers and, as everything that is new, my ads attracted attention.

"That journalist wrote a beautiful article under the heading, 'The Church Without Spire or Belfry.' In it he told how Frank E. Campbell, knowing New York to be a homeless city and one-third of its population to live in hotels, rooming houses, institutions or apartments, all unfitted for the housing and the care of the dead, founded an institution where the dead may lie; not in cold, bare rooms, not alone without attendants, but in homelike surroundings, amongst men and women who care; at a place where the family and their friends may come at any hour, day or night, and make the 'Church Without Spire or Belfry' their home while their dear one is there.

"He told of names, famous in science, art, literature and commerce, of professional men and men of finance, of people of every land and nation, of every creed and of those without belief; for the Church is non-sectarian, dedicated by all religious denominations.

"A few years later, the last rites over the Tribune writer's remains were held in the place he loved, which often he had visited, and which he had named 'The Funeral Church.'"

Since that story has been written, The Funeral Church has a greater, a better home, Broadway at 66th Street, with a chapel still on 23d Street. A beautiful church—still without spire or belfry—a church of pure gothic design, fills the entire second floor of two buildings. The third and the fifth floors of the same two buildings contain private suites, parlors, individual rooms, all beautifully furnished; rooms of different sizes to supply the need of all those who, in this homeless City of ours, recognize the need of a place like The Funeral Church.

Here is an example of another interesting Frank E. Campbell ad:

> **OPEN DAY AND NIGHT.**   **Telephone Connection.**
>
> # FRANK E. CAMPBELL
> **BURIAL AND CREMATION CO.**
> **WORLD WIDE KNOWN UNDERTAKERS**
> *Nos. 241-243*
> # 23d STREET WEST,
> **STEPHEN MERRITT**
> (The) Embalming Inst. of N. Y. (Inc.)
>
> **TELEPHONES:** 1324 Chelsea, Private Exch.   **CABLE:**
> 1325 Chelsea, Gen. all Depts.   Funerals, N. Y.
>
> N. B.—The above establishment and management alike enjoy international reputation. Every service for bereaved, every facility for the care of the dead. No funeral too elaborate, extensive, or moderate. Chapels, parlors, vaults, showrooms, all on premises. Men and women embalmers. Always open.

If the reader will notice in this ad the name of Stephen Merritt appears and under Merritt's name "The Embalming Institute of New York." Prior to the split between Campbell and Merritt the two men had started their own embalming school, which they named after the better known funeral director Stephen Merritt. However, when the creditors lowered the boom on Rev. Merritt, and Frank E. Campbell ended up with the West 23rd St. facility, the name of the "Stephen Merritt, The Embalming Institute of New York" went along with the creditor deal, so Frank E. Campbell ended up being able to use the name of "Stephen Merritt" legally. This did absolutely nothing to improve the already tense relationship between Rev. Merritt and Frank E. Campbell.

By 1910 Frank E. Campbell could boast a staff and payroll of one hundred people.

6. FRANK E. CAMPBELL AMBULANCE

Frank E. Campbell tackled the ambulance service with the same creativity and innovation that he tackled any other project in his life.

Frank E. Campbell initiated a much improved automobile ambulance service in New York City. The services of a Registered Nurse were provided and this nurse went on every ambulance call that was received. Also, the ambulances at Frank E. Campbell's were exclusively Pierce-Arrows (at the time one of the finest automobiles manufactured), and Frank E. Campbell advertised that he offered these vehicles.

Frank E. Campbell was the first to make exclusive contracts with government agencies for ambulance service. He furnished ambulance service for all the immigrants who came through Ellis Island who were handicapped or ill. For a time Frank E. Campbell was the exclusive second tier ambulance provider for the famous Bellevue Hospital (second tier meant that if all of Bellevue's ambulances were on calls and another ambulance need arose, Frank E. Campbell would be first called.). Frank E. Campbell also provided ambulance service for the entire Port of New York which was in itself mammoth in its sheer magnitude. The agreement with the Port of New York included furnishing ambulance service for all the dock workers, ship workers, ship yard workers and passengers for every port in every borough of New York City.

Frank E. Campbell also introduced ambulance attendant uniforms. Eventually he required all of his funeral home staff to present themselves to the public in identical formal uniforms.

FRANK E. CAMPBELL'S AMBULANCE ADS
NOTE HE USES ONLY "PIERCE-ARROW" VEHICLES

THIS WAS THE COMBINATION "PRIVATE AMBULANCE"
AND "CASKET WAGON" OF FRANK E. CAMPBELL.
THE VEHICLE WAS ELECTRIC.
IT RAN ON FOUR BATTERIES AND HAD A TOP SPEED OF
37 MILES-PER-HOUR WITH A 70 MILE RADIUS, WHICH WAS
PERFECT FOR NEW YORK CITY.

7. PROFESSOR LINA D. ODOU

Throughout his long and eventful career Frank E. Campbell took chances on people. He gave people chances, and he gambled on their successes. One of the most interesting of these individuals that Frank E. Campbell took a chance on was a young woman named Miss Lina D. Odou.

LINA D. ODOU

The life and times of Lina Odou is clouded in mystery. Very little is known of her early life, and even less is known about the years following her eventful and rocky association with both Rev. Stephen Merritt, and Frank E. Campbell. In the end she seems to have simply vanished.

In describing Lina Odou it is best to start with describing her vision concerning the professional care of the dead. Lina D. Odou conceived and promoted the concept of having women exclusively embalm the bodies of deceased women and children. It was a 19th century breach of etiquette for a grown man to see a deceased woman or child in a state of disrobe, and hence, this new idea intrigued many in the funeral profession.

When Ms. Odou arrived in New York City she began her work to fulfill this dream. In short order Ms. Odou was able to connect with and persuade both Rev. Stephen Merritt and Frank E. Campbell to help her. With their support Ms. Odou succeeded in founding the only school in history to exclusively train and educate women embalmers. The exclusive female embalming institution also had an all-female faculty.

Ms. Lina Odou was born in 1853. She came from Spain. Her father was an official in the foreign diplomatic service. Eventually Ms. Odou's father was posted in London. It was in London that Ms. Odou met a formidable woman named Miss Florence Nightingale who would change her life. Florence Nightingale is remembered today as the much honored and respected founder of the modern nursing profession.

Florence Nightingale took Ms. Odou under her care and tutelage. At this time the nursing schools in London were considered to be some of the best in the world, and it was in London Ms. Odou received her nursing training. Ms. Odou attended two prestigious institutions: St. Bartholomew and Queen Charlotte's hospitals. Later Ms. Odou attended advanced nursing training at the Vienna College hospital in Austria. It is impressive that Ms. Odou attended three separate nursing programs and even with this record, in the end her aggregate time spent in formal academic nursing education did not amount to one calendar year. The average nursing program at the time was 90 days in length.

When France and Prussia went to –war in 1870, Ms. Odou served as a battle-field nurse with the International Red Cross. After the war, Ms. Odou returned to London.

Ms. Odou's career in nursing advanced quickly and in time she became the preferred nurse for various European royal families. Ms. Odou served as the private nurse to members of the British Royal family, to the family of the Czar of Russia, and finally to the royal family of Italy.

Ms. Odou's brother, who was suffering from tuberculosis, had immigrated to America settling in rural South Dakota where it was thought that the drier climate would offer a much sought after treatment for this deadly disease. It was when Ms. Odou came to visit her unhealthy brother that she made her first trip to America.

It must have seemed to Ms. Odou upon her arrival in the rough and tumble life of South Dakota that she had landed on another planet!

The time Ms. Odou spent in frontier South Dakota was much too harsh for her and the weather she found to be brutal. After her brief stay in South Dakota, Ms. Odou traveled back to New York City where she found a position as a nurse at a New York hospital. At this position her nursing skills and administrative talents soon won her the coveted position as the head nursing supervisor of the entire hospital.

One afternoon while walking the streets of New York Ms. Odou became lost, and ended up on the lower East Side of Manhattan in one of the worst areas of the city, a place known as "The Bowery." The lyrics of an old familiar American song, "The Bowery" describes possibly what Ms. Odou may have encountered on her quiet walk on the streets of old New York.

> Oh! The night that I struck New York
> I went out for a quiet walk
> Folks who are "on to" the city say
> Better by far that I took Broadway
> But I was out to enjoy the sights
> There was the Bow'ry ablaze with lights
> I had one of the devil's own nights
> I'll never go there any more
>
> The Bowery! the Bowery!
> They say such things and they do strange things
> On the Bowery! The Bowery!
> I'll never go there any more

Walking through the streets of "The Bowery" Ms. Odou might have been quietly humming the lyrics of this old song, but what she encountered left her shocked. The utter blight, poverty, and squalor that she witnessed on her accidental trip to "The Bowery" left her heart sick, and there and then resolved to do something – something at least, she thought, to help the unfortunate children.

The intelligent and highly motivated Ms. Odou, at her own expense, established one of the first free standing kindergartens in New York City. Over her life, and particularly during her New York residency she devoted her time and money to caring for the poor and unfortunate children of the city.

It was around the turn of the 19th century to the 20th century that Ms. Odou became first inspired and then obsessed with the idea that women should embalm women and children. Ms. Odou reasoned that just as there were female nurses for women and children, there should be female "nurses" for the dead, and specifically for the dead who were children and women.

Being inspired by her role model Florence Nightingale, Ms. Odou took her philosophy of nursing and applied it to the philosophy of ethically caring for the dead who were women and children.

Ms. Odou's reasoning went this way: Why should the loving care given by a women to another who is sick, even dying, end at death? Why should only men be available to embalm and care for the dead of both sexes? Why shouldn't women be available to carry the duties of care for the patient in death as well as in life?

There was one problem: Ms. Odou did not know how to embalm a dead human body. This impediment did not slow Ms. Odou down at all.

Warmed and motivated by her own enthusiasm for her "new idea" Ms. Odou crossed the Atlantic returning to Europe where she studied under two European authorities on anatomical embalming. The first of her embalming professors was Dr. Edouard Bugnion of Lausanne, and the second was Professor Sigismond Laskowsky, professor of anatomy at the Medical School of Geneva. Both of the highly regarded embalming professors had written extensively on the subject of the art and science of embalming. Ms. Odou was under expert instruction.

PROF. SIGISMOND LASKOWSKY PROF. EDOUARD BUGNION

THE EMBALMING PROFESSORS OF MS. LINA D. ODOU

With her learning and work complete in Europe, Ms. Odou again returned to the United States and became the student of renowned Dr. Auguste Renouard.

Dr. Renouard is remembered in the annals of funeral service history as being the founder of embalming education in the United States. Following her studies with Dr. Renouard, Ms. Odou then obtained employment with the prestigious Boston undertaking company of J. S. Waterman & Sons where she further perfected her skills in the art and science of embalming.

Ms. Odou returned to New York City where she enrolled in Professor A. Johnson Dodge's traveling embalming school, known then as the Massachusetts School of Embalming. The sessions, which were taught by Professor Dodge, were being held in the facilities of the Stephen Merritt Undertaking Company, at the West 23rd Street location.

The education Ms. Odou received from Prof. Dodge was her final course of study in her embalming academic preparation. It was while attending Prof. Dodge's lectures in the Merritt facility that Ms. Odou first met the two men, Rev. Merritt and Frank E. Campbell, who would accept her idea and launch her on her career. Later, however, both gentlemen would turn on her and both men would enter into fierce competition with her.

FRANK S. WATERMAN **PROF. A. JOHNSON DODGE**

Just how Ms. Odou got her foot in the door with both Rev. Merritt and Mr. Campbell is speculation. However, within the legends of the funeral service profession it is told that Ms. Odou persuaded Rev. Merritt to open an embalming school for women and children at his establishment, and that Frank E. Campbell (Merritt's manager) assisted her in convincing Merritt that the idea was a good one.

No matter how this happened, in 1899 the professional journals in funeral service proclaimed a new idea: the establishment of the "New York School of Embalming for Women, at the Stephen Merritt Burial Co.

Note: A word about children and death in 1900. While today this statistic startles people it is nonetheless true: in 1900 out of 1000 babies born, 140 of them would be still born (neonatal death) and 150 of them would be dead in their first year. *The infant mortality rate in 1900 was 290/1000. In 2017 the infant mortality rate in the United States is 6/1000.*

The first class of ten graduated on May 10, 1899. The Commencement exercises took place in the evening at the Stephen Merritt establishment on West 23rd. Street. The Rev. Stephen Merritt gave an inspirational commencement address which everyone agreed was outstanding.

> **NEW YORK**
> **School of Embalming**
> **FOR WOMEN,**
> at Stephen Merritt Burial Co's. 241-3 W. 23d St.
>
> DR. C. H. LE FEVRE, President.
>
> M. S. ROBINSON, Secretary,
>
> Ladies ready to respond to calls from the profession.
>
> L. D. ODOU
> Lecturer and Demonstrator.
> Graduate of European Schools.
> U. S SCHOOL and MASS COLLEGE OF EMBALMING Boston.

After this first graduation ceremony the concept of women embalmers exclusively performing the delicate tasks of embalming women and children swept across the funeral profession in this country. No respectable American undertaker would be so bold as to crudely advertise the services of a "lady embalmer." The idea of a lady embalming the dead was just too much for the public prudish attitudes, but there was no problem or hesitation by hundreds of undertakers in gently promoting and advertising the much softer and delicate moniker of the services of a "lady assistant." From the turn of the 20th century to the mid 1950's every self-respecting funeral director in America offered the service of their own "lady assistant."

Here is an example of Ms. Odou's concept of a "lady assistant" being promoted by a funeral home in their community.

> **HOUSKE FUNERAL HOME**
> Lady Assistant
> Complete Ambulance Service
> Crookston, Minn.   Phone 442-J

Many times the "lady assistant" proved to be the undertaker's spouse, but it made no difference to the public. The public responded to, then and now, a women's presence when death entered their lives.

Ms. Lina Odou's vision proved correct. Her vision contributed to and enhanced a level of gentle ethical care of the dead; before that, the pioneering work of Ms. Lina Odou had been basically unknown in most American communities.

At this point Rev. Stephen Merritt was once again in trouble. This time the reverend clergy went over the line: he had a severe physical altercation with none other than Ms. Odou herself!

What actually started the assault is unclear, but what is certain is that there was a brutal fisticuffs between Reverend Merritt and Ms. Odou. The sparing match between the two former colleagues became so violent that Rev. Merritt, using brute physical force, ejected Ms. Odou from the building. Merritt used so much force the result was that Ms. Odou's arm was severely injured.

Because of this physical assault Ms. Odou suffered great pain in her injured arm for weeks and later she even underwent a surgical operation.

And yet again, the Rev. Merritt got sued. This time by Ms. Odou. No record can be found as to how this law suit was resolved, but speculation is that Rev. Merritt simply settled the matter out of court. However, what the good Rev. Merritt lost, Frank E. Campbell gained, as Ms. Odou, and probably with good reason, now associated herself with Frank E. Campbell The Funeral Church.

By now the West 23rd Street building was being occupied by the Frank E. Campbell Burial and Cremation Company, and Frank E. Campbell now had Professor Odou successfully on the premises conducting her school for woman embalmers.

Frank E. Campbell was no slouch when it came to promotion, and with Ms. Odou in his circle, he made the most of the new opportunity.

Mr. Campbell took every advantage of his new embalming professor's celebrity status in New York City. Frank E. Campbell promoted Ms. Odou's reputation anywhere and everywhere he could.

In national funeral service journals and New York newspapers statements from Mr. Campbell spoke glowingly of Ms. Odou as being not only as the founder of the "Odou Embalming Institute" but he even promoted her as the "Superintendent of the Women's Department of the Frank E. Campbell – The Funeral Church."

In 1902 Ms. Odou married. She married another embalmer by the name of Lewis Zechetto.

After 1905 Mrs. Zecchetto (Lina D. Odou) just vanished. One rumor claimed she returned to Europe. Another rumor had her living on the West Coast. From a verifiable factual standpoint the fate of what happened to one of the funeral service professions most interesting pioneers, Ms. Lina D. Odou, is still a haunting mystery.

8. 66TH & BROADWAY

The history of the career of Frank E. Campbell the man, has at is central core the tremendous success that he had at this address: 1970 Broadway, better known as Broadway & 66th Street. From 1915 until Frank E. Campbell's own death in 1934, great things happened at this address in Midtown New York City.

Here is the story of the Frank E. Campbell - The Funeral Church, at Broadway & 66th Street.

By 1914 it was clear that the old 23rd street building was obsolete. For one calendar year Campbell scouted out properties throughout in Manhattan as a suitable location for his new funeral home.

In 1915 he found what he wanted at 1970 Broadway – the cross street was 66th Street on the West Side of Manhattan.

It was in this building that Mr. Campbell was to strengthen his hold on what was to become a flagship funeral firm in the world.

The 66th and Broadway location was a mammoth building five stories high and two stories underground, with a second attached building housing his floral shop called "Roseland." Greek revival architecture dominated the exterior which featured huge arched windows and plentiful fancy stone work.

**FRANK E. CAMPBELL "THE FUNERAL CHURCH"
NOTE THE SIGN SAYS "BERLIN, PETROGRAD, LONDON" - TRULY INTERNATIONAL. IF A PERSON ANYWHERE IN THE WORLD WANTED TO CABLE CAMPBELL'S THROUGH THE TELEGRAPH THE ONLY ADDRESS THEY NEEDED TO USE WAS: "FUNERALS – NEW YORK"**

For 23 years the Frank E. Campbell - The Funeral Church remained at Broadway and West 66th Street.

To any visitor in those days it must have been an awesome experience to have entered that marvelous facility. Frank E. Campbell had a taste for impressive elegance, and often times throughout his eventful career it was suggested that he even open up an interior decorating department as part of his business interests. Throughout the latter part of his career Frank E. Campbell was even consulted as an interior decorator for some of the wealthy families who resided in Manhattan.

The 66th & Broadway location was a veritable gallery of priceless objects of both art and furnishing. On the walls were hung priceless tapestries and heavy ornate French period furniture, exquisite artwork, heavy draperies of the finest velvet, thick handsome carpets and marble statues from the Roman/Greco era dominated the rooms.

The décor of the funeral home was unlike any funeral home of the time.

Mr. Campbell used soft, mellow lighting in order to assist in removing the basic dark gloom of the "typical" funeral of the period.

On the first floor of the Broadway facility there was a grand reception hall which was designed and constructed from the finest solid Italian marble available. This grand hall was given added dignity by a series of massive Greek columns that ran the entire course of the facility.

Mr. Campbell also installed the first self-service elevator in New York City. What in the world is a self-service elevator? Before this Campbell innovation, every public elevator in New York City had individual elevator operators, and these elevator operators became famous in American slang for asking the questions, "Floor please?"

At the Campbell facility the public only had to ask the first floor receptionist which floor and/or which slumber room their loved one and/or friend was reposing in, and the person just took the elevator up themselves by simply pushing a button – no elevator operator was needed.

The Frank E. Campbell organization was also known for their strict policy in hiring only those people who came to them well recommended in prior employment, and as individuals who were polished, professional, courteous and above all sensitive and caring. Mr. Campbell was a strict task master and he was also known for dismissing staff members on the spot for any breach of etiquette or dress.

Another touching fact about Mr. Campbell's generous attitude towards life was even though The Funeral Church was often described as a palace of royal proportions, Frank E. Campbell, no doubt by recalling his own impoverished childhood, made it a strict company policy that no one, absolutely no one would ever be turned away from The Funeral Church because of financial difficulties. Frank E. Campbell knew from his own life experience that the notion of "the worthy poor" was a living breathing reality – even in New York City – particularly in New York City.

One of the primary reasons as to why Frank E. Campbell, The Funeral Church attracted and maintained the loyalty of the funerals of the theatrical community, on and off Broadway in New York City, is that Mr. Campbell, who himself loved going to the theater, would consistently give away a funeral service to any down and out actor who had died and had no money. Mr. Campbell's generosity to the New York City theater community was never forgotten.

The guests and visitors at Frank E. Campbell, The Funeral Church were always given a map of the entire building which showed the locations of rest room facilities, slumber rooms, relaxation lounges, offices, etc.

All of the slumber rooms at the Broadway facility were given formal names such as "The Renaissance Slumber Room" or "The Louis the XV Slumber Room" or "Library Slumber Room."

The chapel at Frank E. Campbell, The Funeral Church was located on the second floor of the building. It was built with the finest mahogany woodwork, and had a seating capacity for 300 people. There were dark mahogany pews resplendent with velvet cushions.

Accenting the chapel atmosphere was a grand Aeolian-Skinner pipe organ, which was a primary focal point of the room. This grand musical addition, known as "The King of All Instruments" was located in the back of the chapel, which made the greatest impression when people were leaving after a funeral was over. Frank E. Campbell even hired his own company male quartet which furnished live vocal music during a Campbell funeral.

THE CHAPEL OF "THE FUNERAL CHURCH" OF FRANK E. CAMPBELL – 66TH & BROADWAY

In the early 1900's, Frank E. Campbell decided to make the transition from horse drawn funeral vehicles to motorized vehicles. True to his nature of demanding only the best in all matters concerning funerals being entrusted to his firm, Frank E. Campbell's first order for motorized funeral equipment was a fleet of Rolls-Royce funeral vehicles. He ordered the finest auto equipment he could find, however, Mr. Campbell was quick to note that he still offered horse-drawn equipment as a backup.

"THE MAN ABOUT TOWN – NEW YORK, NEW YORK"

Not only was Frank E. Campbell dedicated to quality enhancements in the funeral profession he was also dedicated to being an active leader in his community.

Here are some examples of Mr. Campbell's community involvement. For 25 years he sponsored a marvelous Christmas program for the sick children who were confined in New York City area hospitals. Mr. Campbell would get ahold of Santa Claus, who would show up unexpectedly, and would pass out very nice presents for all the little ones. Then there would be a very professional Christmas pageant.

Mr. Campbell's Christmas pageants were actually small Broadway theatrical productions. The legitimate stage actors, singers, entertainers, producers and directors on Broadway never forgot Mr. Campbell's generosity when one of their own had died and so, when Mr. Campbell asked for acting help he got it. For years actors from the various Broadway theaters in Manhattan donated their services to help make these generous programs grand successes.

Then of course there was the 4th of July. Frank E. Campbell had been born on the 4th of July, and he would never let anyone forget this historic fact. As a consequence of this both his birthday and his observance of the birthday of the United States on the same day, the event became an annual block party. The Campbell home in Larchmont, New York opened to the public and was the social center for celebration and festival. Frank E. Campbell held an open house, complete with free food and free beer along with an impressive fireworks spectacular after the sun went down. Everyone was invited and everyone seemed to show up.

**THE RESIDENCE OF FRANK E. CAMPBELL
LARCHMONT, NEW YORK**

Frank E. Campbell was also an active member of the New York City Rotary Club. The Rotarian's held their meetings at the New York Athletic Club. On the 4th of July, in addition to his open house at his private residence, Mr. Campbell would also dress up as "Uncle Sam" and along with a friend who dressed up as the English "John Bull", the two would present a program on American Independence

Mr. Campbell also created the Frank E. Campbell College Scholarship program which offered free college tuition to needy but deserving writers, play writers, actors, musicians and other young talented individuals who wanted to establish a career in the fine arts.

9. FRANK E. CAMPBELL – THE MAN

Today the name of Frank E. Campbell carries with it a sense of the mystic, a mystery, a riddle. People ask "What was Frank E. Campbell like as a human being?" His name is certainly well-known, but what was he like?

Most native New Yorker's will recognize the Frank E. Campbell name, but few of them can tell you much more than his name is in prominent gold letters and attached over the front entrance of the famous building today on the corner of 81st and Madison Avenue.

What then was Frank E. Campbell like?

By all accounts Frank E. Campbell was a cheerful, friendly, a typical hail-fellow-well-met person with an infectious laugh; he was fun to be around. Mr. Campbell also loved practical jokes, and was usually the entertainment, and master of ceremonies at many social functions. Frank E. Campbell was popular, he had many friends, but, surprisingly few intimates and his marriage was not a happy one.

Mr. Campbell genuinely liked people. His relaxed managerial style in running the funeral company made for good labor relations. One observer said that "Frank E. Campbell rowed to shore with muffled oars."

Some of his employees were with him for decades.

Another interesting aspect of Mr. Campbell's biography is that he was well liked by other funeral directors in New York City, and one of his best friends was Walter B. Cooke, who himself had countless funeral locations throughout the boroughs of New York City.

The story, which might well be apocryphal, says that Mr. Campbell and Mr. Cooke enjoyed meeting at various New York drinking establishments for cocktails, and it was during one of these private get-togethers that the two men decided on their mutual approach to funeral service. It was alleged that Mr. Cooke was determined to go after "the mass" and Mr. Campbell was determined to go after "the class."

Regardless of whether this story is true, it is a fact that this is precisely what happened throughout both men's careers. The firm of Walter B. Cooke catered to the average citizen of New York City, in fact in the 1920's Walter B. Cooke advertised a complete funeral for $250.00 which he boldly advertised, whereas Frank E. Campbell catered to New York's rich and famous and never advertised prices.

Frank E. Campbell was truly humble and it was a humility that sprang up from his total devotion to being of good help and service to others.

One negative in Mr. Campbell's life, however, was his unhappy marriage. Mr. Campbell had married Miss Amelia M. Klutz, from Saugerties, New York in 1905. Mrs. Campbell had been a school teacher in New York City when she met Mr. Campbell. This marriage produced one son, Frank E. Campbell, Jr., who died in the 1960's. While Mrs. Campbell was intimately involved with the funeral company, it is also true that Mr. and Mrs. Campbell lived separate lives, their only mutual interest appeared to be their common love of anything which was beautiful and elegant.

Then there was his mother. Possibly because of his unhappy marriage, Frank E. Campbell became even more devoted to his mother Malvina. In a word, the son treated his mother like a queen. The dutiful son tended to his mother's financial needs while she still lived in Illinois, and after he brought her to live in New York. However, the details of Malvina Campbell's life story are illusive.

However, when Mrs. Campbell celebrated her 82nd birthday in 1923, her dutiful son closed down The Funeral Church for the afternoon. Then, as if that were not enough, Frank E. Campbell even had her broadcast her own personal birthday message to her friends. This broadcast was made on radio station WJZ where the "Campbell Quintet" also made their weekly hymn singing broadcasts. Frank E. Campbell was so excited about his mother's birthday that he actually took out this ad in the Brooklyn Daily Eagle to announce her upcoming birthday broadcast. Such is a son's love for his mother!

> **A BIRTHDAY TRIBUTE**
>
> AS a mark of respect the Frank E. Campbell Funeral Church, Inc., Broadway at 66th Street, will close this forenoon during services and benediction offered at churches of various denominations for the continued good health and happiness of Mrs. M. T. Campbell, mother of Frank E. Campbell, on this, her 82d birthday.
>
> Mrs. Campbell's personal birthday message to her friends will be broadcasted from W J Z radio station during the day.

In addition to his devotion to his mother Frank E. Campbell had one consuming hobby – he raised purebred St. Bernard dogs!

10. CREATIVITY AND INNOVATION

From the beginning of his career Frank E. Campbell had been an advocate of cremation. Not only did his funeral company endorse and encourage cremation, Mr. Campbell was the first funeral professional in the United States to offer scattering of cremated remains at sea and in the air.

In 1916 Mr. Campbell was invited to give the keynote address to Aeronautical Society of America's annual meeting where he explained the benefits of using airplanes for the disposition of cremated remains from the air.

Frank E. Campbell also used his "Hourglass" yacht as a combination funeral coach and passenger vessel for the bereaved. Campbell used the "Hourglass" throughout the waterways surrounding the City of New York. The funeral home staff would put the casket on the vessel, which provided seating, and the staff would serve refreshments for the bereaved as the mournful group traveled to one of the port cities throughout the water ways which surrounded the island of Manhattan.

The "Hourglass" yacht was in the command of Captain Ira Adams. This vessel was sixty-five feet long and had an engine capable of 400 horsepower. The "Hourglass" was no ordinary yacht. It was rumored that the vessel cost $400,000.00, but Mr. Campbell poo-pooed this ridiculous idea saying that the newspapers added too many zeros. The vessel, Mr. Campbell admitted, cost more like $40,000.00. The "Hourglass" was docked at the exclusive Larchmont Yacht Club of which Mr. Campbell was an active member.

According to Frank E. Campbell this "floating funeral home" was good for the public in that it lessened transportation costs on the ground, and it also bypassed traffic congestions in New York City. In an interview Mr. Campbell said, "Railway rates necessitates double fares for body shipments, and party of relatives can accompany, with comfort, the remains to a port near the final burial grounds."

Mr. Campbell also emphasized in his promotion of his floating funeral home that using the yacht offered his clients and guest's fresh air and a moving panorama of scenery which is a positive stimulus in coping with the sadness of mourning, and this environment, Mr. Campbell suggested, is much preferred over the confined, noisy and dirty railroad coach.

The Frank E. Campbell floating funeral home was capable of hosting an actual funeral service on board, and Mr. Campbell installed a small pipe organ for this purpose. The public loved it!

Eighty years before websites and live streaming that allows people thousands of miles away to actually watch and hear a funeral service, Frank E. Campbell installed in the funeral facility at 66th & Broadway an actual radio broadcasting studio WJZ (same radio station where his mother broadcasted her birthday proclamation) whereby the funeral of any decedent using a The Funeral Church could be broadcast across the boroughs of New York right into a person's living room. Mr. Campbell had his own dial on the radio, and every Sunday morning he sponsored a program called "The Frank E. Campbell Hymn Hour" where, you guessed it, the Campbell Quartet would sing old familiar hymns. The public loved it!

Frank E. Campbell also inaugurated the first scattering of human cremains from the air. The cremated remains of Mrs. Sarah D. Brown, a well-known temperance advocate and writer of children's stories, were scattered from Campbell's own private seal plane over the area surrounding the Statue of Liberty. The ashes were scattered to the winds along with nine white carnations and two red carnations, representing Mrs. Brown's age of 92 years by a Campbell staff member. Frank E. Campbell was piloting the plane.

FRANK E. CAMPBELL'S "FLYING HEARSE"

WORLD WAR I AND THE INFLUENZA EPIDEMIC 1917 – 1920

Later in his life, Frank E. Campbell said that the years between 1917 and 1920 were the busiest years of his entire career, and with good reason. Between the onslaught of deaths created by the First World War, and then the subsequent deaths created by the horrible influenza epidemic, which caused approximately 500,000 deaths, every undertaker in the United States was overwhelmed from sun up to sun down.

11. A DAY AT THE FUNERAL CHURCH

There was no question that Frank E. Campbell was successful, however his success did not come without a price. Not everything was perfect, things went wrong and there were failures, disappointments and surprises. The day to day management of The Funeral Church was not in the least an easy proposition.

Here are several examples of a day in the life of The Funeral Church.

In the midst of prohibition the Frank E. Campbell automobile hearse, which was being driven by Richard Norton, a Campbell employee, was stopped a whopping five times by prohibition agents on a trip from Islip, Long Island into Manhattan.

Mr. Norton was in truth actually bringing a decedent to the funeral home, but the first group of prohibition agents were convinced he was smuggling bottles of alcohol inside the casket. Smuggling alcohol this way was not uncommon. It was a trick that bootleggers did routinely to smuggle alcohol into the thousands of New York City speakeasies.

The first group of prohibition agents demanded that Mr. Norton open the casket. Mr. Norton refused, told the agents that Frank E. Campbell had a strict rule that absolutely no casket would ever be opened while being transferred by one of his funeral coaches. Mr. Norton, after a lot of talking, convinced these agents that Mr. Campbell would be terribly upset if a casket was opened on the highway. These agents let Mr. Norton go.

About five miles further at Amityville Mr. Norton was stopped yet again, and again the same thing happened – Mr. Norton talked his way through this one also. Then at Brentwood another group of prohibition agents halted the hearse, and the same thing happened. Mr. Norton was then stopped again in Lynbrook, and again in Long Island City by prohibition agents.

It was at the road stop in Long Island City that Mr. Norton finally had had enough and put his foot down hard. Mr. Norton once again explained to the fifth team of prohibition agents that it was Mr. Frank E. Campbell's firm rule that no hearses or caskets from The Funeral Church were to be opened in-route while transporting a decedent. Mr. Norton went on to tell the prohibition agents that Mr. Campbell felt such behavior was being disrespectful to a human being who could no longer defend their own dignity.

When Mr. Norton finally made it back to Broadway & 66th St. Mr. Campbell was absolutely furious and called the major New York newspapers to report the incident. Frank E. Campbell promised the reporters who came to investigate this very odd story that he would protest directly and in person to the United States government against the actions of the prohibition agents. It is not known whether he acted on his threat.

Then there were the difficult and tragic clients.

In one instance Mr. Campbell was issued a summons from the Magistrate Court of New York City, which was brought by another New York City funeral director accusing Mr. Campbell of removing the remains of a prominent physician from Davenport, Iowa without permission.

This ended up being a simple incident of an arguing family where one family member called Frank E. Campbell, and another family member, unbeknownst to the other family member, called a second funeral director.

Then there were members of the cloth who took exception to Mr. Campbell's approach to running The Funeral Church. One Sunday a clergy person in New York City actually gave a sermon denouncing Frank E. Campbell to the entire congregation from the pulpit. The Rev. George S. Pratt tore into the funeral protection certificate option that Mr. Campbell was offering to the public. The protection program was nothing more than a guaranteed funeral protection plan. It appears that Frank E. Campbell did not respond to the crusading clergy person, but the story did make the New York City papers.

However, there were lighter moments in a day in the life of The Funeral Church.

One day a young Danish couple seeking a church in which to be married were walking aimlessly down Broadway. They were hopelessly lost, and had only been in Manhattan a matter of hours. Just by chance they walked by The Funeral Church and came in. In broken English they asked the receptionist if a clergyman was in; they obviously thought the place was an actual church. The couple continued, in their broken English, to tell the receptionist of their desire to be married immediately.

The receptionist paged Frank E. Campbell immediately, and in short order Mr. Campbell appeared and was utterly thrilled that the couple wanted to get married.

Fortunately, the young couple had all the necessary legal paperwork, and even more fortuitous was that an Episcopal clergy had just finished officiating at a funeral, and after Frank E. Campbell cornered him and asked him to do the wedding the surprised clergy agreed to perform the wedding.

The young Danish couple knew absolutely no one, so Frank E. Campbell ordered the entire Campbell staff to halt what they were doing and attend the wedding. Frank E. Campbell walked the bride down the aisle and gave her away. One of the embalmers on staff served as the best man.

After the ceremony was over the bridal pair were rushed to the train in one of the funeral limousines, courtesy of Frank E. Campbell, to start their honeymoon trip to, of course, Niagara Falls.

It was reported that the staff at Campbell's put together a hastily made bridal bouquet, and they even found enough old shoes and tin cans to tie to the bumper of the limousine so that all New Yorker's could easily recognize the newlyweds as they made their way to the train station. The newspapers reported that for just about fifteen minutes the staff at Frank E. Campbell's "forsook their solemn calling to join in the happy going away."

Then there is the story of Frank E. Campbell's "Undertaker's Green Dinner."

A municipal election in New York City ended up with the candidate that Frank E. Campbell had supported losing, and Campbell's candidate lost by a wide margin. While most people who had invested both time and money in this failed campaign were unhappy and grumbling, Mr. Campbell took the loss in typical good cheer. In fact, Mr. Campbell was such a gentleman loser and good sport that he hosted a dinner for all the losers like himself whose candidate had lost!

It was during this particular election that Mr. Campbell had made a good natured bet with another business man in New York, betting that Campbell's favorite candidate would win.

This dinner was held to serve as a formal ceremony whereby Frank E. Campbell, with a smile on his face, would repay his friend the money he owned him by losing the election bet.

The dinner was arranged at a famous New York restaurant.

The "Undertaker's Green Dinner" event made the newspapers!

FRANK E. CAMPBELL AT RIGHT, SMILING AT HIS "UNDERTAKER'S GREEN DINNER"

At the dinner Frank E. Campbell not only formally paid his bet, but treated the winner and some eighteen other losing friends to a grand banquet. The other losing guests included several clergy and several funeral directors.

Green was the theme. Beginning with the decorations, everything was green. The waiters wore boutonnieres of green flowers, and the menu cards were printed in green.

The first course of the dinner consisted of Green Bay oyster cocktail, with green peppers, and the last entry on the card was green Chartreuse. The party favors were small green dragons. Even the orchestra that Frank E. Campbell had arranged for played "The Wearing of the Green."

In a formal ceremony Frank E. Campbell paid his bet using "greenbacks" and it was claimed that Mr. Campbell was "green" with envy in losing the bet in the first place.

When Babe Ruth, who loved to eat bananas was hospitalized, Frank E. Campbell set a fruit basket made up entirely of bananas to the hospital where the famous baseball player was staying. Frank E. Campbell even sent his famous "Campbell Quintet" over to sing the widely popular song at the time "Yes, We Have No Bananas." Witnesses claimed that Babe Ruth laughed so hard that tears were running down his face, and that he clapped so hard he almost fell out of his bed.

Then, at The Funeral Church, there were some strange and tragic incidences such as the fate of a certain Mr. Frank Mauser.

Mr. Mauser was a silversmith from Newark who on one spring day walked into the foyer of The Funeral Church and asked if the funeral home did business with Woodlawn Cemetery in the Bronx. Mr. Buckingham, who was the General Manager, assured Mr. Mauser that they did indeed work with The Woodlawn Cemetery. It was then, in the middle of this conversation that Mr. Mauser collapsed; he was dead when he hit the floor.

The Coroner was called, and it was determined that Mr. Mauser had swallowed poison out on the street in front of the building, on Broadway, right before he walked into the funeral establishment. On the remains of Mr. Mauser, the Coroner found a note stating that he wanted only Frank E. Campbell personally to handle his funeral, and is stated also the clear intent to literally die in the funeral home reception hall.

The sons of Mr. Mauser were called, and in the end The Funeral Church oversaw Mr. Mauser's funeral, with burial in The Woodlawn Cemetery.

12. GOOD WORKS

For all the professional challenges that Frank E. Campbell confronted there was also the opportunity to be actively involved in good works in the community.

Frank E. Campbell was in the Masonic orders. He was involved with Consistory, Chapter and Commandary, Royal Arch Masons, Scottish Rite (32nd Degree) and York Rite. He was also an active member in the 24th Avenue Methodist Episcopal Church, and served for years as an officer in the Mecca Temple of the Shrine.

When the old Madison Square Gardens was going to be demolished, Mr. Campbell was very concerned about the fate of the famous Saint-Gauden statue of the "Goddess of Huntress" which stood on top of this famous New York City landmark. No one seemed to want the famous statue, so Frank E. Campbell stepped forward and offered to purchase the statue and donate it to the City of New York with the idea of it being placed near the New York City Hall. New York City officials declined the offer, Madison Square Gardens was demolished, and unfortunately the Saint-Gauden statue disappeared and has never been found.

However, what might be described as Frank E. Campbell's finest characteristic was his unbending and unyielding belief in the value, purpose and benefit of funeral rites, rituals and ceremonies.

Frank E. Campbell put this belief into quiet action.

Frank E. Campbell was the first funeral director in New York City to see to the proper disposition of the unclaimed and indigent dead in New York City. For all the grandeur as to his reputation for being of service to the rich and famous, he also gave just as much attention to being responsible for the decent civilized disposition of the poor and disenfranchised.

Mr. Campbell would also accept "unclaimed" cremated remains. Once a year hundreds of these "unclaimed" cremated remains of the lost and lonely in New York City would be interred in several large bronze urns at Mr. Campbell's own expense.

At these sad services, which were public, Mr. Campbell arranged for the representation of both Jewish and Christian clergy, and he furnished beautiful flowers for the occasion.

The other unknown, concerning this selfless service to seek out and take on the responsibility to see to the decent care of New York's "unclaimed" dead, was that Mr. Campbell would only consent to continuing to do this kindness under the strict conditions that he personally and his funeral company in particular received no publicity.

REVERENCE FOR THE DEAD

It is clear that because of these acts of selfless services that the ethic of reverence for the dead held a position of great importance in the life and work of Frank E. Campbell.

For instance Mr. Campbell's ire was raised in 1924 when he learned that the tomb of the Pharaoh Tut-Ankh-Amen had been discovered in the Valley of the Kings in Egypt and that, in Mr. Campbell's opinion, the grave of this ancient leader was being desecrated and destroyed all in the name of archeology.

While the rest of the world seemed to be in an archeological frenzy over this discovery, Mr. Campbell sent a letter to the local New York newspapers under his signature commenting on this event. A portion of this letter is worth quoting: Frank E. Campbell wrote, "It is not pleasant to contemplate the prospect of having the bodies of Washington and Lincoln dug up after a couple hundred or thousand years and being placed on display in a public museum. It is no less revolting to think of a similar indignity inflicted on the last earthly remains of King Tut-Ankh-Amen."

It is a true irony, as we will soon see, that Frank E. Campbell's own remains were left unattended without benefit of grave or tomb for over 70 years.

13. VALENTINO

RUDOLPH VALENTINO
1891 - 1926

The silent movie actor Rudolph Valentino did not live in New York City. The matinee idol was in Manhattan to attend a showing of his new movie "The Son of the Sheik." Valentino had lived in New York City at one time but at the time of his death he was calling Los Angeles his home.

The death and funeral of Rudolph Valentino changed American popular culture as we know it today.

Before Valentino there were famous silent movie performers such as Douglas Fairbanks, and Mary Pickford, but the time had not yet arrived when movie "stars" would have fan clubs, be stalked by the press and the public and have every aspect of their lives reported in breath taking minute to minute segments.

The death and funeral of Rudolph Valentino opened up the celebrity Pandora's Box of public obsession with people now called movie stars and this fascination has never ended.

Three facts are now clear: First is that the public's obsession with movie people had been simmering for some time before Valentino's death, and second is the fact that Frank E. Campbell had no idea of what he was getting into by handling Valentino's funeral. Third, Frank E. Campbell could not have possibly known that the national consequences of what was happening right in front of The Funeral Church would change the American popular culture forever in the creation of the of a new personality, the "movie star."

As you will soon read Mr. Campbell himself later described Valentino's funeral as being INSANE!

Prior to the death of Rudolph Valentino when popular actors and actresses died, their funerals were not the media frenzy and excitement and drama that Valentino's death elicited.

In fact, Rudolph Valentino had another funeral later in Los Angeles, but his funeral on the West Coast paled in comparison to the ceremony held in Manhattan. The question can be asked why? Why was the New York City funeral of Rudolph Valentino such a game changer?

One answer might possibly be the massive population of New York City, and the totally unexpected death of the silent movie idol. New York City had a population 5 times larger than Los Angeles in 1926, and when the news of Valentino's death hit the press the New York public "en masse" went crazy, and they went crazy inside and in front of Frank E. Campbell's The Funeral Church.

Also, Rudolph Valentino defined a new genre in American popular entertainment – the sex symbol. Other handsome male actors had graced the silver screen, but it was Rudolph Valentino who captured the sexual allure that had been repressed in the American culture for decades. Rudolph Valentino was Hollywood's original "Latin Lover." Women worshipped Valentino, and men were either threatened by his persona or wanted to be like him.

Another point to make is that

by the time of the funeral of Rudolph Valentino, Frank E. Campbell had been diagnosed with terminal heart disease. Mr. Campbell had only a few years to live. Today, looking back over the veil of time, it is clear the "insane" grand funeral ceremony that was afforded Valentino would be Frank E. Campbell's high-water mark in his long and eventful career.

Here is what happened.

At the time of the untimely and unexpected death of silent movie star Rudolph Valentino the reputation for funeral service excellence that Frank E. Campbell, The Funeral Church enjoyed had already been cemented into the psyches of not only New Yorkers, but in the minds of Americans across the county.

And in 1926, when Rudolph Valentino died, The Funeral Church was already the best known funeral company in America.

While The Funeral Church most certainly had taken care of most of the most famous people in New York City, and while The Funeral Church had indeed conducted much larger and much more complicated funeral services throughout its history, it was the funeral of silent movie star Rudolph Valentino that has commanded the attention of countless authors, documentarian, historians and most of all the American public throughout the last 90 plus years

On August 15, 1926, Valentino collapsed at the Hotel Ambassador on Park Avenue in Manhattan. He was hospitalized at the New York Polyclinic Hospital. Following an examination, he was diagnosed with appendicitis and gastric ulcers, and surgery was performed immediately. (His condition was referred to as "Valentino's syndrome"-- perforated ulcers mimicking appendicitis.) After surgery, Valentino developed peritonitis. On August 18, his doctors were optimistic about his prognosis. The media was told that unless Valentino's condition deteriorated, no updates would be given. However, his condition worsened on August 21. He was stricken with a severe relapse of pleurisy, which developed rapidly in his left lung due to his weakened condition.

Valentino's physician, Dr. Harold G. Meeker, realized that Valentino was going to die, but as was common at the time, chose to withhold this information. Valentino reportedly believed that he would recover. During the early hours of Monday, August 23, Valentino was briefly conscious and chatted with his doctors about his future, but soon lapsed into a coma. A Roman Catholic priest was called in to administer Last Rites. He died a few hours later at 12:10 p.m. at the age of 31.

When Rudolph Valentino died Frank E. Campbell was on his yacht "The Hourglass" conducting a funeral onboard. When the funeral home called him he returned to Manhattan immediately. For the next three days Mr. Campbell would get no sleep, and later he would describe the events surrounding the death and funeral of Rudolph Valentino in one word "INSANE!"

Two funeral directors arrived at the Polyclinic Hospital to transfer Valentino's remains back to Broadway & 66th Street. The funeral directors placed the silent movie star's remains in a plain wicker basket and then they covered the basket with a cloth of gold. Large crowds of people had already gathered at the West 51st entrance to the hospital, and in a short time a squad of New York City Police officers were dispatched to control the growing and extremely restless crowd. When the crowd realized that Valentino's remains were on their way to The Funeral Church this same crowd quickly regrouped on Broadway right in front of the entrance to "The Funeral Church." The chaos had begun, and would only get worse as time went by.

Once Valentino's remains were at the funeral facility the body was prepared and embalmed. However, funeral arrangements were still incomplete. For a time no one actually knew who was in charge.

The staff at The Funeral Church were besieged and the decision was made to bolt all entrances to the building. The first night was quiet and a twenty-four hour police guard was positioned at all the entrances of the building. All this would change over the next several days.

As dawn broke over New York City, it was estimated that 100,000 people lined the streets of Manhattan to pay their respects.

In London, England, when Miss Peggy Scott found out about Valentino's death, she committed suicide by drinking poison. She left a suicide note which read: "I am only a little butterfly made for sunshine and I cannot stand loneliness and shadow. With his (Valentino's) death my last bit of courage has flown. I feel I have been stretched for years like a piece of elastic." Miss Scott claimed to be a friend of Valentino's, but at the coroner's inquest no proof of that claim was forthcoming. She ended her sad epistle with these maudlin lines, "In 1922 Rudolph helped me carry on. He told me a lot of his own sufferings. Perhaps it was only a matter of time anyway before the elastic snapped. I have had wonderful moments with him. There's a lot I cannot tell you." She ended with this haunting sentence, "Please look after Rudolph's picture for me."

In New York City, and in other cities and places, other suicides and attempted suicides of despondent fans were reported.

> **MILLIONS PAY LAST TRIBUTE TO DEAD IDOL**
>
> Crowds Clamor for Last Look at Valentino Remains, Lying in State

The first day of public homage it was estimated that between 50 – 75,000 people filed by the bier where Rudolph Valentino reposed. Mostly things were quiet.

Around 11:40 p.m. the crowd inside and outside became unruly. Suddenly the front windows of The Funeral Church were smashed as fans tried to get in. Valentino's body was laid out on a bronze catafalque in "The Gold Room." As the agitated and tense crowd now passed through "The Gold Room" the staff confronted a terrifying problem. Nearly half of these "mourners" in line were trying to steal some type of souvenir - anything; the unruly crowd was ruining The Funeral Church itself.

The crowd was stopped at the entrance door of the funeral home and the remains of Valentino, for safety sake, were removed to a small room which was considered much more secure, and once again The Funeral Church was bolted down for the night.

An all-day riot erupted on August 25. Over 100 mounted officers and NYPD's Police Reserve were deployed to restore order. A phalanx of officers lined the streets for the remainder of the viewing time. An actress, Pola Negri, from Poland, now claiming to be Valentino's fiancée, collapsed in hysterics while standing over the coffin. It was estimated that over 1000 people tried to storm The Funeral Church.

In this utter chaos people were trampled by the police horses. As the police pushed the crowd back onto Broadway a score or more of people lurched or fell against a parked automobile overturning it – the car caught fire.

By this time Broadway looked like a disaster area. Confusion reigned. Women yelled and screamed in fright and ducked for protection from the crowd, automobiles and the mounted police. The New York City Police Commissioner himself arrived at the scene but was unable to influence any calm.

RUDOLPH VALENTINO IN STATE IN "THE GOLD SLUMBER ROOM"

SCENES FROM THE FUNERAL FOR SILENT MOVIE STAR RUDOLPH VALENTINO

THE HEADLINES ON THE FRONT PAGE OF
"THE NEW YORK WORLD"

CROWDS LINED UP AT FRANK E. CAMPBELL "THE FUNERAL CHURCH" TO VIEW THE REMAINS OF RUDOLPH VALENTINO

Finally, out of desperation, the Police Commissioner gave the order for the mounted police patrol to charge the crowd in a last desperate attempt to establish law and order.

It was about 2:30 in the afternoon when the police horses charged the crowd. By this time it was evident to the police and Campbell's staff that the majority of the rebellious people were what were dubbed "repeaters." In other words, these rowdy folks were not sincere mourners but instead were merely curious. It was noted in the press that these rambunctious people didn't even look sorrowful and they most certainly were not reverent.

The results of the mounted police charge was disastrous. There were scores of injured. People suffered fractures of bones, received lacerations, contusions and head injuries.

Frank E. Campbell sent out his own ambulances to carry the injured to the various hospitals, and he called additional funeral home ambulances to help with the disaster.

Frank E. Campbell was right: the funeral for Rudolph Valentino was "INSANE!"

Rudolph Valentino's funeral mass in Manhattan was held at Saint Malachy's Roman Catholic Church, often called "The Actor's Chapel", as it is located on West 49th Street in the Broadway theater district, and has a long religious association with show-business figures.

After Valentino's remains were taken by train from New York to

California, a second funeral was held on the West Coast, at the Catholic Church of the Good Shepherd in Beverly Hills. Valentino had no final burial arrangements and his friend June Mathis arranged a temporary solution when she offered a crypt that she had purchased for the husband that she had since divorced. Coincidentally, she died the following year and was interred in the adjoining crypt that she had purchased for herself; Valentino was never moved to a new location and he remains in the crypt next to Mathis. These two people are still interred side-by-side at Hollywood Forever Cemetery (originally Hollywood Memorial Park Cemetery) in Hollywood, California.

The funeral for Rudolph Valentino would be the last spectacularly grand celebrity funeral that Frank E. Campbell would conduct.

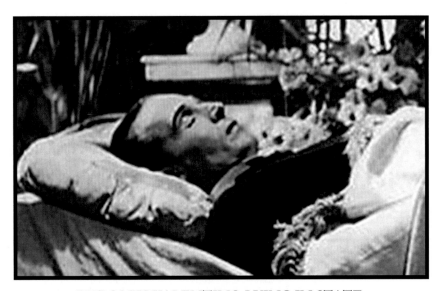

RUDOLPH VALENTINO LYING IN STATE

14. THE FINAL DAYS

From 1930 until his death in 1934 the health of Frank E. Campbell steadily declined. As already mention he had been diagnosed with heart disease before the Valentino funeral, and over time he became weaker and weaker until by 1932 he was not even going into the office.

Mr. Campbell spent most of his time at his home in Larchmont. Over were the block parties, over were his participation in so many charitable and civic activities in New York, and over were his years of creativity and innovation.

On January 9, 1934 Mr. Campbell was admitted to the Post-Graduate Hospital in New York City, and died quietly around 4:00 p.m. on Friday, January 19, 1934. He had lived 61 years, 6 months and 15 days.

His remains were immediately taken to The Funeral Church where they were prepared for the funeral and entombment ceremonies.

It was estimated that over 3000 people came to pay their respects while Mr. Campbell lay in state.

> **In Memoriam**
> **Frank E. Campbell**
>
> In the death of Frank E. Campbell, I feel a deep sense of personal loss, for he was a friend of many years. Our profession loses one of its leading members, ever active in raising standards of service; and our community is the poorer through the passing of this fine and generous citizen.
>
> CHARLES ROSENTHAL, Founder.
>
> **RIVERSIDE MEMORIAL CHAPEL**
> *Where Beauty Softens Grief*
> 76th St. and Amsterdam Ave.
> ENdicott 2-6600

The New York newspapers were effusive in their praise of his life and career. The New York Times announced in big bold black type that **"FRANK E. CAMPBELL UNDERTAKER, DIES."** The obituaries were filled with statements such **as "ARRANGED 25,000 SERVICES" and "DIRECTED RITES FOR NOTABLES HERE DURING THIRTY-FIVE YEARS OF BUSINESS CAREER."**

The death notices also were complete with giving an impressive inventory of accomplishments that Mr. Campbell had completed during his career. Testimonies were recounted about his deep belief in advertising, his innovation in adopting motorized funeral cars, his dislike of anything morbid, and his establishment as the most attractive and beautiful funeral establishment in New York.

The obituaries also noted the many famous people he had buried such as Frank W. Woolworth, Oscar Hammerstein, and of course, Rudolph Valentino.

The newspapers also gave tribute to Mr. Campbell's keen sense of humor and dry wit, and gave attention to the fact that he was not averse to poking fun at himself and at his profession now and then.

Mr. Campbell's body lay in state beneath a screen of flowers resting in a massive cast iron bronze casket which weighed in excess of 1800 lbs. Over 3,000 persons came to The Funeral Church to pay their respects.

The funeral was held from the chapel at The Funeral Church with about 500 people in attendance, and virtually every funeral director in New York City was in attendance.

FRANK E. CAMPBELL WAS ENTOMBED IN THIS CAST IRON BRONZE CASKET

A Presbyterian and Episcopal clergy officiated and the service was brief and simple. Prayers were read, the congregation joined in reciting the Lord's Prayer and a soloist sang the Ava Maria.

Then Frank E. Campbell left 1970 Broadway, and his beloved The Funeral Church that he had founded for the last time. His remains were transported across the Hudson River to the Mausoleum at the New York & New Jersey Cremation Company. Just why Frank E. Campbell purchased mausoleum space at this particular place is unknown. What is known, however, is that Frank E. Campbell would not rest in peace!

15. REST IN PEACE MR. CAMPBELL - ???

It is a sad, strange and ironic tale to tell concerning the bizarre course of events and journey that the sacred remains of Frank E. Campbell and his mother experienced following both their deaths. In a word, they both were left unattended and uncared for in a side store room in the basement of the mausoleum where the crypts spaces were at, for over 70 years.

When the body of Frank E. Campbell arrived at the mausoleum in New Jersey, it became clear that due to the size of the massive cast iron bronze casket it would not fit into the mausoleum crypt. In fact, when Frank E. Campbell's mother died in 1926, her cast iron bronze casket, which was even larger than his, would not fit either. For some strange reason Frank E. Campbell himself did nothing about this – could it be he didn't know about his mother's casket being too large?

Hence, neither of them, mother or son, were ever placed in their rightful mausoleum spaces. Instead both decedents were rolled into an empty storeroom in the basement of the mausoleum and it was there that they remained – for years!

In 2001, Mr. Eugene Schultz, the President of Frank E. Campbell at the time, now called "The Funeral Chapel" instead of The Funeral Church, decided to correct this indignant situation and through his magnanimous efforts both Frank E. Campbell and his mother were finally interred in The Wood Lawn Cemetery in the Bronx, which is one of the most prestigious and beautiful cemeteries in the world. Just why this happened to the remains of Mr. Campbell and his mother will probably never be known.

Frank E. Campbell, Jr. was involved in the operation of the funeral establishment for a while, then he sold the firm and moved to Florida where he died in the 1960's.

Today the Frank E. Campbell, "The Funeral Chapel" is still a thriving presence on the corner of 81st and Madison Avenue in Midtown New York City.

16. MR. CAMPBELL'S GHOST

In writing the account of the life and career of Mr. Frank E. Campbell, who is just possibly might be the most famous funeral director ever, I have been asked by several people this question: "What do you think Frank E. Campbell would do today given all the massive changes that are happening in funeral service?"

In researching this fascinating man's life I now have an answer for this question. However, before I share my answer please allow me to disclaim the notion that I have a crystal ball, or some kind of inside information, or have held a séance where I have spoken with Mr. Campbell, or that my response to this question might even be right.

With this disclaimer and confession I will give the reader my answer.

I feel that Frank E. Campbell would once again be leading the charge straight into the world of funeral service creativity and innovation in a nonconformist way, and with vision and courage, and turning a blind eye to the critics.

Just think about that combination a moment: courage and nonconformity. One compelling example in Mr. Campbell's career to back this position up is this: Is it not fascinating that a single human being could dream up and then create and implement such an innovative thing called "The Floating Funeral Home?" Think about this a moment. Frank E. Campbell accomplished this over ninety years ago, and I would suggest that in 2017 Mr. Campbell would be no more of a shrinking violet now when confronted with all of the religious and cultural changes that contemporary funeral professionals in this country face every day.

I have concluded that if Frank E. Campbell were alive today his image would be gracing the front cover of every professional. He would also be coming up with one new funeral enhancement idea after another, and he would muster the courage that even if the ideas were deemed "crazy" by some, he would turn a blind eye to ever present naysayers who want to argue any new idea to the point that they kill it.

Any funeral professional who can create "The Floating Funeral Home" has courage, and what is even more important for us to learn from Mr. Campbell progressive ideas is that while there were certainly the negative critics, overall, and in general, the public loved what he offered.

The good news is that here and there, just every now and then, once in a while I meet a modern day Frank E. Campbell out in the world of our beloved profession in 2017. In fact, I leave some meeting and conversations with the feeling that Mr. Campbell's ghost is still haunting a few outstanding funeral homes, and a few outstanding funeral professionals.

I believe that Frank E. Campbell is still a beacon of exemplary funeral service excellence that we who love our profession can be inspired from, learn from, and most importantly, imitate in our day to day devotion to this great profession.

Frank E. Campbell believed passionately in the value, purpose and benefit of the funeral. So might be said of us.

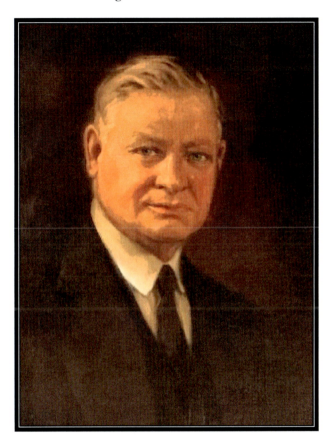

Frank Ellis Campbell
Funeral Director Extraordinaire

17. EULOGY

In Greek the letters "eu" mean good, and the letters "logos" means word. When "eu" and "logos" are put together and you have the word "eulogy" which translates into a "good word." It is fitting and proper that this work concludes with a good word about Mr. Frank E. Campbell.

What then can the final assessment of the life and career of Frank E. Campbell be? When Mr. Campbell died, many in New York commented that he was one of the best men in the city.

It's hard to find people who are truly good, decent, hard-working, kind-hearted, and humble – but Frank E. Campbell was all of these things.

Frank E. Campbell loved being a funeral director, and the results of his career bears out the truth of his professional attitude.

Two of the stellar qualities of Mr. Campbell, as odd as this might sound were these: He did not take himself that seriously, and he learned somewhere along the line the priceless life lesson that the only way to be truly happy is to be of service to other people – and without question Frank E. Campbell lived this life goal of being helpful and of service to others with a consistency that few people ever attain in a lifetime.

Mr. Campbell had conducted the funerals for kings, princesses, counts, barons, baronesses, actors, actresses, clergy, politicians, statesmen, entertainers, producers, directors, dancers, publishers, and the meek and poor of New York City.

It was said of Mr. Campbell at his death that he was great. That may be true, but as impressive as it is to be great, it is even greater to be human, and Frank Ellis Campbell possessed a great and grand humanity about him. He wanted to help people. What higher calling?

RESOURCES

Journals:
Casket & Sunnyside
The Casket
The Funeral Director's Review
The Mid-Continent Mortician
The National Funeral Service Journal
The Northeast Funeral Director
The Western Undertaker

Newspapers:
Middletown Times-Press – Middletown, New York
The Brooklyn Daily Eagle
The Evening World – New York, New York
The Evening Telegraph – Buffalo, New York
The New York Herald
The New York Sun
The New York Times
The New York Tribune

Websites:
www.maplegrove.biz/
https://www.findagrave.com/
www.churchtimeline.com/

Public Records:
Merritt Burial Cremation Co. V. Merritt Co. 1913
https://casetext.com/case/merritt-burial-cremation-co-v-merritt-co/
The New York Public Library
The New York State Library
Russell Sage College Library

Additional Resources:
Mr. Charles S. Salomon
Frank E. Campbell, The Funeral Chapel

ABOUT THE AUTHOR

Todd W. Van Beck has been serving the funeral profession for fifty years. He started his career at the Heafey & Heafey Mortuary in Omaha, Nebraska and throughout his career has been involved with every aspect of the purpose, meaning and benefit of funeral rituals and ceremonies, as well as the subjects of death, grief, bereavement care, funeral service history, as well as management issues in funeral service. Mr. Van Beck is an author, teacher, lecturer on an international basis. He has published over 600 professional articles as well as having written over 60 training programs. His book "Winning Ways" was published in 1998, and most recently he has published two new books, "Reverence for the Dead" and "The Story of Cremation." He was honored by the ICCFA Educational Foundation with their first "Landmark Career" award in 2014. Mr. Van Beck also holds an honorary doctorate degree from the Commonwealth Institute of Funeral Service. He is currently on the staff of the John A. Gupton College, in Nashville, Tennessee. He is married to Georgia who is a Clinical Supervisor with Hospice.

Made in the USA
Middletown, DE
06 October 2018